Green-Up Kids

Protecting the Planet, One Project at a Time!

A Handbook for the Next Generation who are passionate about protecting our planet, its people, and the animals!

By C S Wurzberger,
The Green Up Girl®

Want to use this Green-Up Kids curriculum in your school, home schooling groups, summer camp, daycare center, library, church, girl & boy scouts, 4-h group, campground, zoo, aquarium, wildlife conservation center, or other?

Contact us at **office@AwesomeAnimalAcademy.org** for bulk order quantities and discounts.

ISBN: 9781689432689

Awesome Animal Academy, C S Wurzberger, 84 Route 100, West Dover, VT.

AwesomeAnimalAcademy.org

This Handbook is dedicated to the next
generation of young people who want to
help protect the planet and truly make
an impact by launching and leading
their own green-up projects!

TABLE OF CONTENTS

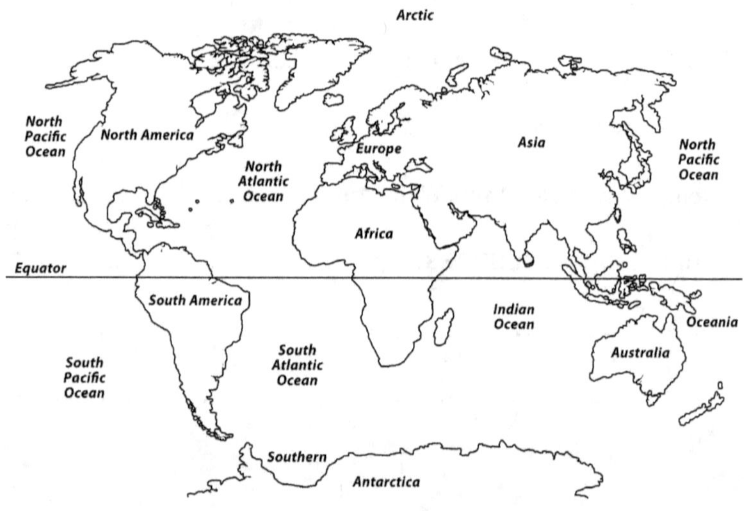

Arctic
North Pacific Ocean
North America
Europe
Asia
North Pacific Ocean
North Atlantic Ocean
Africa
Equator
South America
Indian Ocean
Oceania
South Pacific Ocean
South Atlantic Ocean
Australia
Southern
Antarctica

INTRODUCTION

In the world of our ancestors, there was an abundance of animals running free and crystal clear waters filled with fish and marine life.

But now our world is filled with mountains of trash both on land and in the oceans. Even remote forests and beaches have traces of human waste. More animals and plants than ever are threatened and on the verge of extinction.

We can do something about this! We can make it better!

This earth is the only home we and the animals have. It's up to us to get together and inspire each other to protect us all.

"The frog does not drink up the pond in which he lives." — **Native American Proverb**

You can have a positive impact in our world! Join youth from around the globe who are starting school gardens, boycotting pesticides to help save pollinators, and so much more.

With the right guidance you too can take your idea, dream, or concept and bring your project to life.

This handbook gives you the inside knowledge, know-how, and resources you need to launch your Green-Up Project™.

Each step brings you closer to achieving your mission!

Dear Green-Up Kid,

Welcome to the world of making a difference and protecting the planet, its people, and our animals.

I'm C S Wurzberger, The Green Up Girl®. Ever since I was a little girl, I've known my life's mission is to inspire people to care for the earth and its animals. I'm so excited to guide you on your journey to launch a Green-Up Project you can be proud of.

My compassion for animals blossomed in the 4th grade when I was asked to select an animal and write a paper for my English class.

As I was flipping through the pages and pictures of a book, I came across the Dodo bird, a funny looking creature that caught my attention.

As I read on, I discovered that the Dodo bird went extinct in 1681 because of over-hunting and the introduction of animals that preyed on its young.

Boy, was I an upset little girl! I thought 'This bird could have been saved if humans had cared a little more."

I remember coming home from school to tell my parents about the tragic news, yet they didn't seem to understand why I was so upset. I stomped my feet and shouted "But we need to care. This bird will never be seen on the earth again."

It was hard for me to understand why no one in my life seemed to understand my passion for animals, and I didn't have the resources to speak up and make a difference.

Well, now I have the resources!

I spend my time passionately speaking up for animals and protecting their natural habitats. I don't want to see any more animals going extinct.

Here are a few things going on in our world:

- Only 27% of plastic water bottles are recycled. The rest end up in the landfills and can take up to 1,000 years to decompose.

- Over 100,000 marine mammals die each year from plastic pollution in the ocean.

- The number of endangered animals have grown 179% in our lifetime alone.

And I know you care, too.

I'm here to help you share your voice, concerns, and visions — and bring your ideas and solutions to the world!

Together we're going to explore the changes you want to see in the world!

In the upcoming chapters of this Handbook, you'll discover how to:

- Explore what you're passionate about
- Bring that vision to life
- Inspire others to join in
- And pull it all together with your Green-Up Project™

What's really exciting about this Handbook is it gives you a detailed direction to ensure your project comes alive and shows you how to create your own Green-Up Project™.

So get ready!

My team and I are here to help you.

Anything you're passionate about can be turned into a purpose-driven project!

How To Make The Most Of This Interactive Handbook

To get the full value of this Handbook, jump in to each section with your wild imagination.

You'll benefit the most if you…

- Read through the entire Handbook one step at a time,

- Complete each set of Action Steps and Worksheets, and

- Prepare to create your own Green-Up Project™.

Completing the worksheets in each chapter will take you a step closer to building your project and following your journey to protecting the things you love.

So, have fun filling out these worksheets!

REDUCE
REUSE
RECYCLE
REPURPOSE
RETHINK

Step 1: PICK A GREEN-UP PROJECT TO LEAD

Begin with the change you want to see in the world!

Here is your chance to clarify your concerns, speak your passions, and share solutions with the world.

In this Step you'll discover how to:

1. Define what you want to improve in the world.

2. Explore the type of green-up project you want to launch.

3. Blast off with your BIG IDEA.

Let's dive in!

Grab a pen, find a comfortable spot, and let's get started!

Or you can download the worksheets at: <u>AwesomeAnimalAcademy.org/green-up</u>

1. **Define What You Want To Improve In The World.**

* **What changes do you want to see?**

* **What messages do you want to share?**

- Who do you want to share the
  messages with?

- Why should other people care?

2. Explore The Type Of Project You Want To Launch.

Sharing your voice and concerns are two of the most exciting aspects of your Green-Up Project™.

This is where your project comes to life.

You can start a school garden, grow a bee friendly garden, stop using palm oil to protect orangutans, and more.

Now it's your chance to explore the possibilities.

Let your eco-brain go wild! There are so many exciting options.

What type of Green-Up Project do you want to launch?

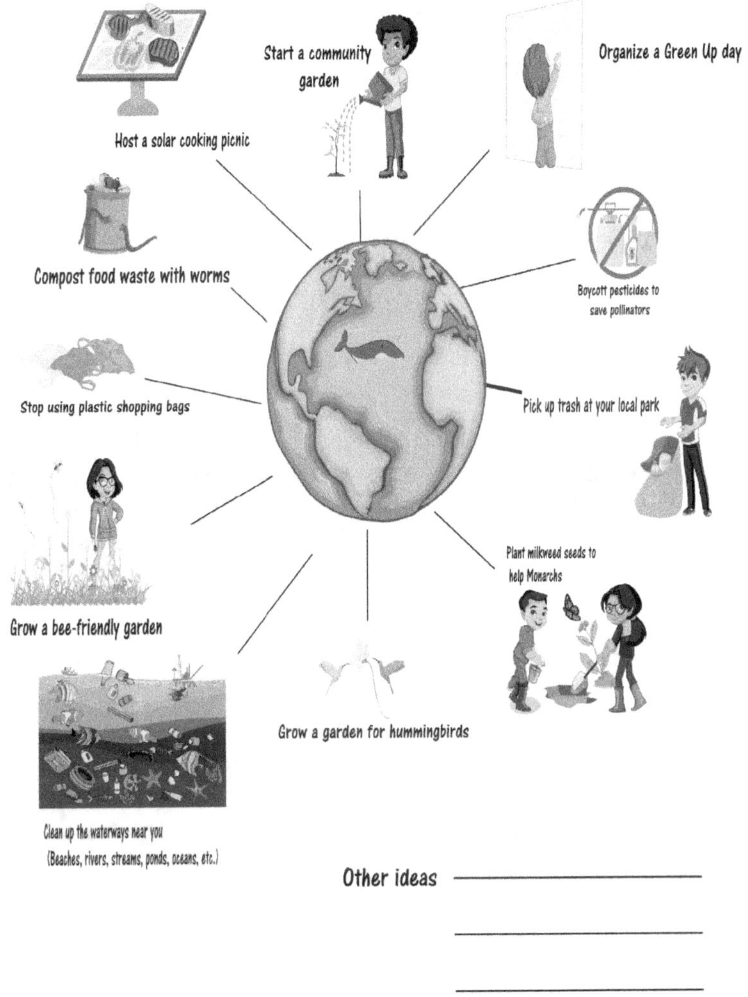

Other ideas _________________________

____

____

3.   Blast Off With Your BIG IDEA.

You've defined the changes you want to see in the world and explored a variety of Green-Up Projects™ you could launch. Now it's time to narrow down your options and choose your BIG IDEA!

A dream that energizes and excites you. An idea that will impact the world, its people, its animals, and even your life.

- **What lights up your soul and makes it smile?**

- **Who do you want to help?**

- **Write your BIG IDEA here:**

- **What are the major issues your project is looking to change?**

- **Why should these issues be addressed?**

STEP 1: Summary—Action Items

Pick A Green-Up Project™ To Lead

Mark off each item on the checklist to ensure you are moving closer to bringing your Green-Up Project™ to life:

- I have defined what I want to improve in the world.

- I have identified my BIG IDEA.

- I have selected my Green-Up Project™.

Congratulations! You have just completed your first step towards bringing your Green-Up Project™ to life.

Things I learned in this section:

Step 2: PLAN AND LAUNCH YOUR PROJECT

Now that you're done brainstorming project ideas and you've clarified your dream direction, it's time to roll up your sleeves and bring your Green-Up Project™ to life.

In this Step you'll:

1. Give your project a name.

2. Get specific with the specifics.

3. Have fun funding your project.

Let's dive in!

Grab a pen, find a comfortable spot, and let's get started!

Or you can download the worksheets at: AwesomeAnimalAcademy.org/green-up

1.   Give Your Project A Name

Naming your project is a very important step. You'll want to choose a name that reflects your mission.

Sit down and give yourself a brainstorming session. Come up with a whole list of names that could easily represent your Green-Up Project™ and try them out on a few potential followers, friends, family members or anyone else you can think of. You'll quickly know if it's going to be memorable and work for you. If everyone says "Huh?", you may need to consider a different name.

- **Make a list of possible names.**

- **Test out the names and narrow down the list.**

Drum roll please! Which name wins?

- **What is the name of your project?**

2. Get Specific With The Specifics

Bringing your BIG IDEA to life requires a look into all the little details that you need to do to make it happen.

Have fun answering the questions that being with…

Who—What—Where—When—How

Use the worksheet to help you organize your Green-Up project.

Bring Your Green-Up Project to Life

For example, if you were creating a community butterfly garden, here are some questions you need to ask yourself:

WHO do you need to help you?
are your team members?

[Example: adult supervisor, a gardener, friends, family, etc.]

WHAT supplies do you need?
[Example: organic seeds, soil, shovels, rakes, spades, gloves, etc.]

HOW will you get the word out about your Green-Up Project™?

WHEN are you planning to start your project?

[Example: Set a specific date. Will it be in the Spring, Summer, or Fall?]

[Example: promotional flyers, advertising, newspapers, press releases, social media, Facebook live, podcast, and more.]

HOW will you make it happen?

Example: Do you need transportation getting there?
Do you need permission from the location?

HOW will you pay for your project?

WHERE is the project happening?

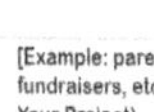

[Example: parents, family members, fundraisers, etc.] (See Step 3: Fund Your Project)

[Example: a school yard, community land, park, etc.]

Now that you've outlined the specifics of your Green-Up Project™ you need to determine how will you pay for your project? If there is a cost. [Example: parents, family members, fundraisers, etc.]

3. Have Fun Funding Your Project

Depending upon what type of project you launch, you may need to raise a little money to help pay for supplies.

Let's start by listing out your project expenses and filling in the below worksheet. (You can also download an Excel or Numbers spreadsheet at: AwesomeAnimalAcademy.org/green-up

For starters, I would recommend you begin with what supplies you need, transportation costs (gas) , advertising (flyers, postcards, etc.).

Here is an example of how to lay out a simple budget. On your spreadsheet you'll want to enter your numbers for the entire project.

Project Name: Butterfly Garden	
EXPENSES:	
Organic Seeds	$10
Garden Soil	$60
Lumber to make raised beds	$55
Total Expenses	$125

Also please note, depending upon your type of project, you may have other expenses like advertising, travel expenses, etc. Now it's your turn to fill in the numbers.

Start by using this spreadsheet to set up your first budget. List all your expenses.

Use the below spreadsheet or download an Excel or Numbers spreadsheet at <u>AwesomeAnimalAcademy.org/green-up</u>

Project Name:	
EXPENSES:	
Total Expenses	

My project will cost:_______________________________

STEP 2: Summary—Action Items

Plan And Launch Your Project

Mark off each item on the checklist to ensure you are moving closer to bringing your Green-Up Project™ to life:

- I have chosen my project's name.

- I have answered the questions WHO, WHAT, WHERE, WHEN, AND HOW.

- I have identified all my expenses.

- I have listed all my expenses in an easy to follow budget.

Congratulations! Now you're ready to inspire others to join in.

Things I learned in this section:

Step 3: PRESENT YOUR GREEN-UP PROJECT™

In this step you'll present your Green-Up Project™ and inspire others to join you.

In this Step you'll:

1. Plan your messaging.

2. Write your press release

3. Present your project's details.

4. Broadcast with a podcast.

Let's dive in!

Grab a pen, find a comfortable spot, and let's get started!

Or you can download the worksheets at: AwesomeAnimalAcademy.org/green-up

Choose what you want to say and share to encourage others to lend a hand.

You can connect with them through press releases, your favorite social media sites, and even with a podcast show.

1. Plan Your Messaging

If you're wanting to generate excitement and followers for your Green-Up Project™ you'll want to choose encouraging words.

Consider what you want to say and share.

The actual words and phrases that you use on each of your promotional materials is important.

Answer the following questions to ensure your messaging resonates with your ideal fans and followers.

- **What is the ultimate reason for inviting people to join you?**

- **How will your project make life better?**

The next important piece is the 3 - 5 sentence pitch describing what your project is all about. This is simply a brief conversation you have with someone to describe your Project in just 5 sentences or less. It is designed to simply spark an interest.

Example: I'm [insert your name] and my Green-Up Project™ is to inspire people to use cloth shopping bags and help protect sea turtles.

Did you know that thousands of sea turtles die every year because plastic shopping bags blow in the ocean and the turtles think they are jelly fish, try to eat them, and suffocate?

Will you join me in boycotting the use of plastic bags? It's simple, you can either use cloth shopping bags every time you shop or request paper bags instead.

The sea turtles and I thank you for helping.

Now it's your turn!

- **Write your project's 3 - 5 sentence pitch:**

2. Write Your Press Release

A press release is simply a story that people write and send to newspapers, magazines, and radio stations.

They are a great way to get people's attention and tell them about important news or special events!

In this section you are going to write one about your Green-Up Project™ and send it to members of your family, friends and classmates.

Your press release will include a headline and a short story about your Green-Up Project™ and why it is important to you.

First you will write the draft and then write the final copy on the next worksheet.

- **Write a headline or story hook** (A title that grabs the readers attention)

- **Write a story describing your Green-Up Project** (Write 5 sentences or more)

3. Present Your Project's Details

* **Where do you want to present your project and who do you want to share this information with?**
(Example: present your plan to your family and/or at school, give a talk at your local library, record your own podcast, be interviewed on the Awesome Animal Academy podcast, and anywhere else you want to share your project).

- **How will you present your Green-Up Project™?** (Example: Do you want to recored a podcast? Do you want to show a slide show? Do you want to create a video to share on YouTube? Etc.).

To make presenting easy, simply fill out the Present Your Green-Up Project worksheet.

Present Your Green-Up Project!

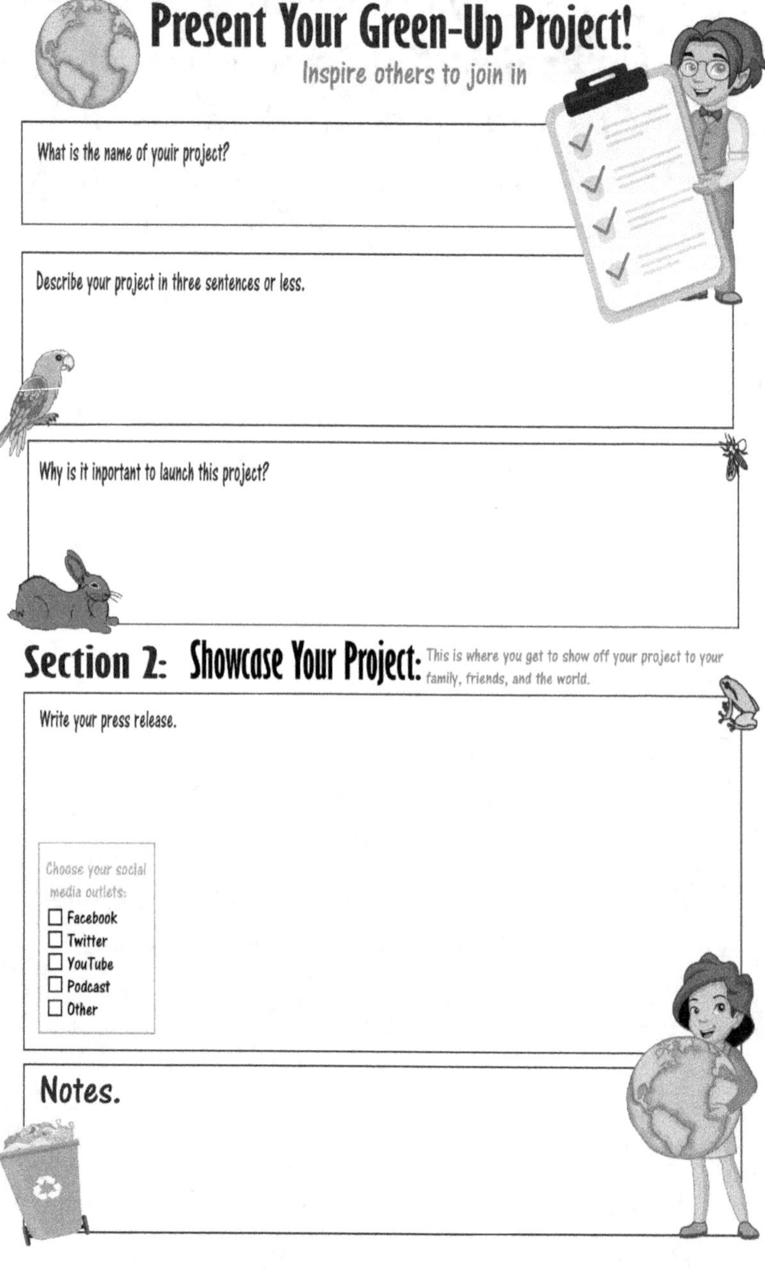

What is the name of youir project?

Describe your project in three sentences or less.

Why is it inportant to launch this project?

Section 2: Showcase Your Project: This is where you get to show off your project to your family, friends, and the world.

Write your press release.

Choose your social
media outlets:
☐ Facebook
☐ Twitter
☐ YouTube
☐ Podcast
☐ Other

Notes.

4. Broadcast With A Podcast

A podcast is simply a free radio/television-like broadcast. You can easily plug in and listen or watch them on your computer, smart phone, iPad, iPod or any media gadget.

The podcasting movement is growing quickly and becoming one of the best ways for sharing your Green-Up Project™ with listeners around the world.

Podcasting is experiencing huge growth with over 575 million active subscribers on iTunes, 315 million mobile device users, and over 8 million downloads on Stitcher.

Here are the 7 key benefits to podcasting:

1. Podcasts are more personal - The content is communicated directly to the listener via audio and video and it's a more intimate way of sharing information compared to reading it from an email, website page, or document. The host becomes a trusted adviser and friend who can make recommendations and guide actions.

2. Podcasts are easy to consume - Podcasts can be listened to and viewed on a smart phone, tablet, computer, or selected cars at the listener's convenience.

3. Podcasts are mobile - They travel where ever you go. You can listen on your morning bus ride to school, walk around the park, on an airplane, while you're in a car, or any other activity.

4. Podcasts are affordable to distribute - They are delivered digitally, no cost for postage, printing, and paper. Plus, you don't have to worry about it getting lost in the spam filter.

5. Podcasts give credibility – When providing expert, engaging content, your audience will see you as an authority and follow your recommendations and guidance.

6. Podcasts can expand your reach quickly via social media - Each Podcast episode can be shared with your social media community and easily passed on to each of your listeners and followers. Plus, it is an easy way to distribute your message quickly and lasts for years to come.

7. Podcasts can deliver amazing results – Unlike many promotional tactics that you can't measure, podcasting is one you can. All downloads are tracked through your hosting company. You'll be able to see daily, weekly, monthly downloads from each episode, what country the listener is in, and what technology they are using to consume your podcast, and many other details.

Get ready to add podcasting to your promotional mix!

You can kick off your own podcast or be a guest on someone else's podcast like Awesome Animal Academy.

To learn how to podcast or be a guest on one of her shows, contact C S Wurzberger at 802-258-8046 or send her an email at office@AwesomeAnimalAcademy.org

Also check out her Handbook, "Broadcast with a Podcast.

You can pick up a copy at amazon.com or AwesomeAnimalAcademy.org/handbooks.

STEP 3: Summary—Action Items

Present Your Green-Up Project™

Mark off each item on the checklist to ensure you are moving closer to presenting your ideas and solutions with the world:

- I have planned my messaging and created my pitch.

- I have decided where to present my Project.

- I have written my first press release.

- I have explored the 7 benefits to podcasting.

- I have decided to record a podcast, or not.

Congratulations! Now you're ready to inspire others to join in.

Things I learned in this section:

YAHOO! YOU DID IT!

You now have a completed Green-Up Project™ and can start protecting our planet.

You must be so proud of yourself. I know I sure am!

I look forward to hearing all about your success stories. Feel free to reach out and I'll also share your project's details on our social media platforms.

Email me at:
office@AwesomeAnimalAcademy.org

Or you can connect with me at:
Facebook.com/awesomeanimalacademy

MORE GREEN-UP ACTIVITIES

Turning Trash Into Treasures

Turn Your Trash Into Treasures!

The average person throws away 4.6 pounds of trash every day. What's really sad is 70% of it could be reused or recycled.

Before you throw an item away.
Take a moment to think about it!

- Reduce the amount you use
- Reuse the items over and over
- Recycle the items into something new

Rethink about the ways your can turn your trash into treasures!

Ideas:
- Turn old milk jugs into bird feeds and watering stations
- Turn coffee cans into storage containers
- Turn Lunchable trays into jewelry boxes

Now it's your turn to Rethink! List out how you can turn your trash into treasures?

How Long Until It's Gone?

Did you know that many of the items you throw away can take many years to breakdown in the landfill? This means we need more and more landfills to hold all of our trash. How sad :-(This means less health land for us and the animals that live on the earth.

Shoes
50-80 Yrs

Cigarette Butt
10 Months to 10 Yrs

Receipt
3-4 Months

Tin Can
200-500 Yrs

Toothbrush
200-500 Yrs

IceCream Stick
1-2 Yrs

Tissue
3 Months

Plastic Bag
450 Yrs

Straw
700 Yrs

Lollipop Stick
450 Yrs

Glass Bottle
4000 Yrs

Chewing Gum
5 Yrs

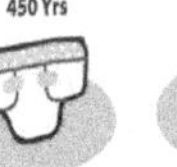

Plastic Beverage Ring
50 Yrs

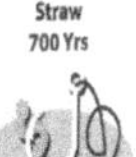

Disposable Diaper
450 Yrs

Fishing Line
500 Yrs

Clothing
1Yr

Apple
A few days to 6 Months

Plastic Bottle
100-1000Yrs

Styrofoam Food
Container
Over 500 Years

Juice Boxes
5 Years

Make a list of other items you throw away and look up how long they take to decompose.

ITEM	HOW LONG UNTIL IT'S GONE?

Composting Food Waste With Worms

Composting Food Waste With Worms

In this activity we are going to put food scraps in a bin with Red Wiggler Worms and watch them compost it into rich, healthy dirt.

Fun Facts About Red Wiggler Worms:

- They are a type of earthworm
- They are the best worms for composting
- They can eat half their weight in food every day
- They have gizzards like chickens to help grind up their food
- They can not bite or sting people

Fun Things To Look Up About Red Wiggler Worms. Record your findings below:

What do red worms like to eat? ___________________

How many worms are in your bin? ___________________

How long are they? How much do they weigh? ___________________

How fast do they eat their food scraps?

____

Record other fun facts:

For more fun, try to find the hidden adult worms, baby worms, and eggs

ADDITIONAL RESOURCES

No need to struggle on your own!

Here are three easy ways to become the leader you are meant to be:

- Attend a live online instructor-led workshop — Green-Up Kids program and discover more ways to protect the planet. Or watch the video replay whenever it's convenient for you. Visit: AwesomeAnimalAcademy.org/event to see the complete schedule.

- Sign up to work privately with C S Wurzberger as your very own personal mentor through programs like Become a Stentor with a Mentor. (A stentor is a person with a powerful voice). Visit: AwesomeAnimalAcademy.org/mentoring

- Bring a group Green-Up Kids program to your school, homeschooling group, young professionals group, library, 4H Club, summer camp, local wildlife conservation center, zoo, aquarium, and more. Visit: AwesomeAnimalAcademy.org

When you need help, give me a call at 802-258-8046 or send me an email at office@AwesomeAnimalAcademy.org

Enjoy making the world a better place for all living creatures!

Did you have fun learning how to launch Green-up projects?

If so, you'll also want to check out my other Handbooks and Programs where you can:

- Save a Species
- Lead Like a Lemur
- Start an Eco-Friendly Business

Here are 3 ways to get started:

1. Buy the Interactive Handbook that sparks your interest.
2. Sign up to take an online course.
3. Attend a live session at Awesome Animal Academy, 84 Route 100, West Dover, VT.
4. Bring a program to your school, library, homeschooling group, and more.

Each session empowers the you with tools you need to succeed in the 21st Century.

Save a Species

K.I.S.S.es for Awesome Animals

This Interactive Handbook is filled with activities for kids who love animals and want to get involved is saving species.

Pick up your copy at <u>amazon.com</u> or <u>AwesomeAnimalAcademy.org/handbooks</u>.

Lead Like a Lemur

An Interactive Handbook that launches young people into the leaders and stewards they are meant to be!

Pick up your copy at <u>amazon.com</u> or <u>AwesomeAnimalAcademy.org/handbooks</u>.

Start an Eco-Friendly Business

Start a Business and Sell Like a Stingray

This Interactive Handbook helps young socialpreneurs bring their business vision to life and take charge of their financial futures.

Pick up your copy at <u>amazon.com</u> or <u>AwesomeAnimalAcademy.org/handbooks</u>.

Each Interactive Handbook and program gives you the know-how to soar and dive deeper into the world of leadership, stewardship, and social entrepreneurship.

Best of all you'll receive all the resources and assistance you need from me and my team!

For more info visit:

AwesomeAnimalAcademy.org/handbooks

AwesomeAnimalAcademy.org/programs

Awesome Animal Activities

Enjoy hours of unplugged fun!

This Awesome Animal Activities book is filled with 49 fun mazes, coloring pages, puzzles, word searches, spot the differences, and much more! Only $4.95

Pick up your copy at amazon.com or AwesomeAnimalAcademy.org/handbooks.

ABOUT THE AUTHOR

"What we appreciate, we preserve.
What we value, we conserve.
What we are taught, we understand.
And when we understand, we can come
together to protect the earth and its animals."
-- C S Wurzberger, The Green Up Girl®

C S Wurzberger
TheGreenUpGirl.com
AwesomeAnimalAcademy.org

C S Wurzberger, The Green Up Girl® is an environmental educator, green movement leader, award-winning Podcaster, author, youth mentor, speaker, and an accomplished Business Growth Strategist with 35+ years of experience. She specializes in working with ambitious and enthusiastic young entrepreneurs as their personal mentor while also guiding them through the whole process of becoming the awesome leaders, stewards, and entrepreneurs they are meant to be!

C S is the Host of three podcasts:

Conservation Celebrations:
This podcast spotlights remarkable conservation projects happening around the world to save animals and protect their natural habitat.

The show unveils the impact of each project, shares details, and celebrates their outcomes. ConservationCelebrations.com

Greener by Choice-Living the Lifestyle: This podcast series engages in conversations, shares simple action steps, and provides resources so you can enjoy living a greener lifestyle. Plus, as a bonus features eco-friendly products, and spotlights green movement leaders who are making a difference all around the world. Let's come together and ensure a greener, cleaner future for all. GreenerbyChoice.com

Awesome Animal Academy: This podcast series is for children, teens, and adults who love animals! Together we explore the lives of rare, exotic, wild and endangered farm animals. Plus, what it means to be a leader, steward, and entrepreneur. AwesomeAnimalAcademy.org

All of the podcasts can be heard on iTunes or directly at AwesomeAnimalAcademy.org/podcasts.

The shows have thousands of listeners and are downloaded in over 75 countries.

C S is also the Founder and Director of Awesome Animal Academy. An organization that offers in person and online leadership, stewardship, and social entrepreneurship programs for children, teens, adults, and educators who love animals and want to make a difference!

The Next Generation is frustrated with all the environmental damages that are being done to our earth and the increased number of endangered animals. They are looking for ways they can step up and help.

Awesome Animal Academy offers hours of unplugged fun through a series of offerings (including coloring books, interactive handbooks, podcasts, project-based programs, and more!).

They help young people build confidence, grow 21st Century skills, strengthen their financial futures, and develop respect and empathy for all.

As a team, Awesome Animal Academy launches young people into the leaders, stewards, and social entrepreneurs they are meant to be!

Located at 84 Route 100, West Dover, VT 05356

Visit <u>AwesomeAnimalAcademy.org</u> .

Appendix
Worksheets, Checklists and Resources to Lead Like a Lemur

Each chapter in this Handbook includes worksheets and they are available at AwesomeAnimalAcademy.org/green-up as 8 1/2" x 11" sheets you can download and work with. You may want to fill them in, print them out and put them in a notebook for easy reference at any time.

Worksheets available for download:

- What type of green-up project do you want to launch?

- Bring your Green-Up Project to Life

- Present Your Green-Up Project

- Turning Trash Into Treasures

- How Long Until It's Gone

- Composting Food Waste With Worms